CRITICAL SPIRIT
Confronting the Heart of a Critic

JUNE HUNT

ROSE PUBLISHING/ASPIRE PRESS

Carson, California

ROSE PUBLISHING/ASPIRE PRESS

The information and solutions offered in this resource are a result of years
of Bible study, research, and practical life application. They are intended
as guidelines for healthy living and are not a replacement for professional
counseling or medical advice. JUNE HUNT and HOPE FOR THE
HEART make no warranties, representations, or guarantees regarding any
particular result or outcome. Any and all express or implied warranties are
disclaimed. Please consult qualified medical, pastoral, and psychological
professionals regarding individual conditions and needs. JUNE HUNT
and HOPE FOR THE HEART do not advocate that you treat yourself or
someone you know and disclaim any and all liability arising directly or
indirectly from the information in this resource.

For more information on Hope For The Heart, visit .
www.hopefortheheart.org or call 1-800-488-HOPE (4673).

Printed in China by Regent Publishing Services Ltd.
March 2016, 4th printing

CONTENTS

Dear Friend,

I've been around both—those who have one and those who don't. And there is no joy when you have to be around someone with a *critical spirit*!

People with a critical spirit are like porcupines: When they feel threatened, they push out their barb-like quills to protect themselves and can deeply stab your heart.

We don't feel safe with *sharp-quilled people*. We know as surely as they can attack others—often without justification—they can just as easily turn on us without provocation.

Unfortunately, those who have a critical spirit don't recognize this negative character flaw in themselves. Instead, they defiantly proclaim, "I'm not negative. I'm just *right*!"

If you try to have a close relationship with someone who has a *porcupine-personality*, realize that it's next to impossible to embrace a porcupine without getting hurt. And then, if you are being subjected to the jabs of an unjust critic, be on guard—you could get into the same negative pattern by jabbing back.

If you have been initiating the barbs, the guaranteed solution to stop you from "barbing" is one profound sentence spoken by Jesus: *"Do to others as you would have them do to you"* (Luke 6:31).

Just imagine, if every person with a critical spirit were to apply this passage every moment of every day, the transformation would be life-changing. No more barbs, no more jabs, no more sharp-pointed quills—just the permanent change of a life reflecting the love of Christ.

Yours in the Lord's hope,

June

June Hunt

CRITICAL SPIRIT
Confronting the Heart of a Critic

"Curse God and die!" The words spew out of the mouth of an embittered wife who is stunned and stymied by tragedy. Gone ... destroyed ... are *all* their possessions and *all* their children as a result of God's allowing Satan to test her godly husband in order to prove his faith.

Job mourns their losses but doesn't malign the goodness of God. Instead he submits himself to the sovereignty of God by declaring, *"The LORD gave and the LORD has taken away; may the name of the LORD be praised"* (Job 1:21).

But *"Curse God and die!"* is her retort, especially after seeing her husband suddenly stricken—afflicted from head to toe with painful sores. She observes this once respected man—so revered in the community—now scorned and reduced to sitting in a pile of ashes and scraping his sores with a jagged piece of pottery. Job's noble stance before the Lord is absolute nonsense to her. She doesn't want to hear one more word of devotion from her disease-ridden husband.

A critical spirit consumes the wife of the one whom God calls *"the greatest man among all the people"* (Job 1:3). However, she's had enough, and she wants Job—and God—to know it! *"Are you still maintaining your integrity?"* she pounds, unleashing her toxic tongue: *"Curse God and die!"* (Job 2:9).

DEFINITIONS

Everything is fine ... until they open their mouths. They are aghast at the sight before them. Their once highly respected friend is now horrifically humbled. Eliphaz, Bildad, and Zophar—let's call them Eli, Bill, and Zo for short—have set out from their homes to pour out comforting words upon their troubled friend, but now they find themselves speechless. For seven days and seven nights they sit on the ground and commiserate, and *"No one said a word to him, because they saw how great his suffering was"* (Job 2:13).

But soon their sympathetic presence morphs into a barrage of stinging rebuke that further crushes the spirit of poor Job. He responds in deep emotional pain ...

> **"Anyone who withholds kindness from a friend forsakes the fear of the Almighty."**
> **(Job 6:14)**

Like Job's friends, has someone in your life assumed the role of your personal *heavenly sandpaper*—a self-appointed expert at finding fault and continually focusing on your faults in an attempt to "refine" you? The abrasive words are not helpful, but hurtful, and qualify as *verbal and emotional abuse.* Such criticism grates against the grain of your soul, wearing you down and stripping you of your worth.

God holds all of us accountable for how we use our words, especially words that wound. Harsh, critical words don't pour out of the hearts of godly people. Jesus said ...

> **"For the mouth speaks what the heart is full of. A good man brings good things out of the good stored up in him, and an evil man brings evil things out of the evil stored up in him."**
> **(Matthew 12:34–35)**

WHAT IS a Critical Spirit?

Eli (Eliphaz), most likely the eldest among the friends, speaks first—ever so cautiously. But then his words take on a presumptive tone. By the time Eli finishes, he insinuates that Job is being disciplined by God because of sin and that the wise way for Job to proceed is to submit to the discipline.

But there's a problem with his critical presumption. Job's tortuous troubles have nothing to do with sin. Instead, they're all about a showdown between God and Satan over his testimony. Will Job stand strong or will he fall? The Bible says ...

> **"Blessed is the one who perseveres under trial because, having stood the test, that person will receive the crown of life that the Lord has promised to those who love him."**
> **(James 1:12)**

At the Wimbledon tennis championship in England, a judge sits on an elevated chair to the side of the net between two competitors. The judge is hired for the prestigious match by earning the reputation for consistent fairness and accuracy. When a ball is served outside the boundary line, the judge yells, "Fault!" These judgment calls are appropriate and appreciated.

The person with a critical spirit, however, hasn't earned the reputation of being accurate or fair-minded. This judge sits uninvited and elevated above others, yelling "fault ... fault ... fault!" These calls are inappropriate and unappreciated.

The Bible is not silent about those who have a critical spirit—those who sit smugly in the judgment seat looking down arrogantly on others.

> **"You, then, why do you judge your brother or sister? Or why do you treat them with contempt? For we will all stand before God's judgment seat."**
> **(Romans 14:10)**

▶ A **critical spirit** is an excessively negative attitude characterized by harshness in judging.

- Criticizers judge others severely and unfavorably.

- Hypercritical people judge others with unreasonably strict standards.

- Faultfinders look for and point out flaws and defects with nagging and unreasonable criticism.

For example, certain circumcised Jewish believers unjustly criticized the apostle Peter for daring to fellowship with the uncircumcised. The issue of circumcision (was it necessary for salvation or not) created sharp division in the early church. *"So when Peter went up to Jerusalem, the circumcised believers criticized him"* (Acts 11:2).

▶ **"Criticism"** comes from the Greek word *kritikos*, which means "able to discern or skilled in judging."[1]

▶ **Criticism** has two different meanings:[2]

- Speaking fairly with discernment in regard to merit or value (A literary *critic* is expected to give a fair critique by accurately analyzing, judging, and reporting.)

- Speaking unfairly with trivial or harsh judgments (A person with a *critical spirit* gives unfair criticism by faultfinding, nitpicking, and quibbling.)

The Bible stresses the powerful impact of our right and wrong words ...

> **"The tongue has the power
> of life and death. "
> (Proverbs 18:21)**

Job's friends initially demonstrate a caring spirit, reflecting the deep, attentive love of God in the midst of suffering.

But then the misguided pride that accompanies a critical spirit consumes them to the degree that the three men are more concerned with delivering theological points than showing desperately needed compassion.

The Bible has much to say about pride, including God's heart attitude toward it.

> " ... I hate pride and arrogance,
> evil behavior and perverse speech."
> (Proverbs 8:13)

One of our deepest needs is for someone to care about us—our successes and failures, our strengths and weaknesses, our virtues and vices. We want people to be attentive to our likes and dislikes, our joys and sorrows, our dreams and disappointments. How blessed we are when we have people with caring spirits in our lives!

But how much more secure we feel when we come to know the breadth and the depth of God's love and care for us.

The apostle Paul said ...

> "I pray that you, being rooted and
> established in love,
> may have power, together with all the Lord's
> holy people, to grasp how wide and long
> and high and deep is the love of Christ,
> and to know this love that surpasses
> knowledge—that you may be filled to the
> measure of all the fullness of God."
> (Ephesians 3:17–19)

▶ **Caring** involves someone giving watchful or painstaking attention based on desiring what is best for others.[3]

- To care means to be thoughtfully attentive and protective.

- To care means to be personally interested in or feeling affection toward someone else.

- To care means to be actively involved in doing what is best for another person.

The One who created you gives loving, *watchful* care toward you. This care is expressed in Scripture ...

> "What is mankind that you are mindful of
> them, a son of man that you care for him?
> You made them a little lower
> than the angels; you crowned them
> with glory and honor."
> (Hebrews 2:6–7)

▶ **Caring** people are genuinely interested in showing concern for others. In the Bible we read about truly caring people.

- The Good Samaritan, who took care of the savagely beaten traveler

  "He [a Samaritan] *went to him and bandaged his wounds, pouring on oil and wine. Then he put the man on his own donkey, brought him to an inn and took care of him"* (Luke 10:34).

- The apostle Paul, who cared for the new Christians young in their faith

  "We were like young children among you. Just as a nursing mother cares for her children ... " (1 Thessalonians 2:7).

- The Christians in Philippi, who sent a brother to care for the needs of Paul

  "But I think it is necessary to send back to you Epaphroditus, my brother, coworker and fellow soldier, who is also your messenger, whom you sent to take care of my needs. ... he almost died for the work of Christ. He risked his life to make up for the help you yourselves could not give me" (Philippians 2:25, 30).

After Eli's speech, Job replies in his own defense, expressing a need for sincere encouragement instead of wounding words: *"My brothers are as undependable as intermittent streams, as the streams that overflow,"* Job laments (Job 6:15). His friends increase his burdens rather than help relieve them. He further responds, *"Now you too have proved to be of no help; you see something dreadful and are afraid"* (Job 6:21).

In truth, from our earliest years, we've all yearned for approval; we have cried out for encouragement. When we learned to write, our hearts called out, "Mommy, look what I drew!" When we were learning to swim or play baseball, our hearts called out, "Daddy, look here! Look at me!" Just as children need encouragement, adults need encouragement too. But not just occasionally—the Bible says we need this regularly.

> **"Encourage one another daily."**
> **(Hebrews 3:13)**

▶ **Encouragement** involves one person inspiring another person with comfort, counsel, and confidence. *Encourage* literally means "to cause another to be confident."[4]

- The prefix *en* means "to cause to be"; *courage* means "confidence."

- The encourager "causes" others to have *confidence* to do what needs to be done and to make needed changes.

- The Lord encouraged Joshua to *"be strong and very courageous"* in leading the Israelites to inherit the land God promised to give them (Joshua 1:7–8).

The Bible says we should all be encouragers.

> **"Encourage one another**
> **and build each other up."**
> **(1 Thessalonians 5:11)**

▶ **"Encouragement,"** translated from the Greek word *paraklesis*, literally means "a calling to one's aid" to give comfort or counsel.[5]

- *Para* means "beside"; *kaleo* means "to call."

- We are called to come alongside and comfort others.

- The Holy Spirit is the "paraclete"—our Comforter, our Counselor, our Advocate.

Jesus said ...

> **" ... the Father ... will give you another**
> **Counselor to be with you forever."**
> **(John 14:16 HCSB)**

> **"The Comforter, which is the Holy [Spirit] ...**
> **shall teach you all things ...**
> **Let not your heart be troubled,**
> **neither let it be afraid."**
> **(John 14:26–27 KJV)**

Throughout the long book of Job, God is mostly silent, speaking only at the beginning and at the end. But make no mistake about it—He doesn't miss a single word of conversation between Job and his three "friends."

Never assume that just because God is silent, He is absent. In the end, He speaks up and reveals His heart response to a critical spirit. *"One who loves a pure heart and who speaks with grace will have the king for a friend"* (Proverbs 22:11).

Jesus came to earth clothed in humanity in order to die for us, but He also came to show us the Father —in human flesh. He did that both by His actions and by His words. Therefore, if we want to know the Father's heart on the subject of a critical spirit, we need only examine the life of Jesus—or the way He behaved toward people and what He said to them. Clearly, He confronted sin in people's lives, but He did it compassionately—not with a critical or condemning spirit. He did it as the Father did it then and as He still does it now.

When it comes to interacting with others, the Lord wants us to examine our own conduct and motives. Jesus spoke unforgettable words with unforgettable imagery: *"Do not judge, or you too will be judged. For in the same way you judge others, you will be judged, and with the measure you use, it will be measured to you. Why do you look at the speck of sawdust in your brother's eye and pay no attention to the plank in your own eye? How can you say to your brother, 'Let me take the speck out of your eye,' when all the time there is a plank in your own eye? You hypocrite, first take the plank out of your own eye, and then you will see clearly to remove the speck from your brother's eye"* (Matthew 7:1–5).

▶ **Don't** be judgmental or you too will be judged.

"Do not judge, or you too will be judged" (v. 1).

▶ **Don't** judge others or you will be judged in the same way and measured by the same standard.

"For in the same way you judge others, you will be judged, and with the measure you use, it will be measured to you" (v. 2).

▶ **Don't** focus on the small faults of others, before focusing on your own big faults.

"Why do you look at the speck of sawdust in your brother's eye and pay no attention to the plank in your own eye?" (v. 3).

▶ **Don't** talk to others about their faults while you ignore your own faults.

"How can you say to your brother, 'Let me take the speck out of your eye,' when all the time there is a plank in your own eye?" (v. 4).

▶ **Don't** be hypocritical—correct your faults! Then you can correct someone else's faults!

"You hypocrite, first take the plank out of your own eye, and then you will see clearly to remove the speck from your brother's eye" (v. 5).

CHARACTERISTICS

Bill (Bildad) can no longer contain himself, he is becoming increasingly frustrated that Job isn't owning up to his supposed "sins" and admitting that God is disciplining him. *"How long will you say such things? Your words are a blustering wind"* (Job 8:2). Bill's compassion erodes into cruelty, and he even accuses Job's children of sinning, and concludes that's why God allowed them to be killed. He makes this tragically wrong presumption ...

**"When your children sinned against him,
he gave them over to
the penalty of their sin."
(Job 8:4)**

Is there someone in your life who has been especially hard on you? Notice how those with a critical spirit seek to cancel out their own "shortcomings" by focusing on their own "good intentions," but they condemn you by focusing on your faults. Faultfinders feel justified in playing dual roles: both *judge* and *jury*. Meanwhile, those being judged feel unjustly criticized, unjustly compared, and unjustly condemned.

God, on the other hand, never calls attention to our faults in a way that wounds our spirit. Instead, His plan is to bring positive—though sometimes painful—conviction for this one purpose: to motivate us to change.

A caring spirit ... where to find it? The bombardment of criticism is getting to Job. He is slipping into despair and growing cynical—even of God and His justice. *"It is all the same; that is why I say, 'He destroys both the blameless and the wicked.' When a scourge brings sudden death, he mocks the despair of the innocent. When a land falls into the hands of the wicked, he blindfolds its judges. If it is not he, then who is it?"* (Job 9:22–24).

Job's desperate discouragement in the midst of righteous tribulation demonstrates the importance of manifesting a caring spirit to those in their darkest hours. We are told to ...

> " ... walk in the way of love, just as Christ loved us and gave himself up for us as a fragrant offering and sacrifice to God."
> (Ephesians 5:2)

Isn't it interesting how differently people handle the same situation—sometimes in completely opposite ways? Two people receive the same bad news—one reacts negatively and the other reacts positively. Two people see someone make a mistake: One person lacks mercy and the other extends mercy.

Those with a critical spirit rarely focus on the needs of others—they're too busy focusing on the faults of others. A critical spirit and a caring spirit are on opposite ends of the spectrum; the one tears people down while the other builds people up.

Nine Distinct Differences

A Critical Spirit	A Caring Spirit
Condemns the person as well as the action	Condemns the action, but not the person
"The words of the reckless pierce like swords, but the tongue of the wise brings healing" (Proverbs 12:18).	
Focuses on the faults of others	Focuses on your own faults
"Why do you look at the speck of sawdust in your brother's eye and pay no attention to the plank in your own eye?" (Luke 6:41).	
Ridicules others	Encourages others
"Whoever derides their neighbor has no sense, but the one who has understanding holds their tongue" (Proverbs 11:12).	
Makes judgments based on appearances	Makes judgments based on facts
"Stop judging by mere appearances, but instead judge correctly" (John 7:24).	
Assumes the worst without first hearing from the accused	Assumes the best while waiting to hear from the accused
"Does our law condemn a man without first hearing him to find out what he has been doing?" (John 7:51).	

A Critical Spirit	A Caring Spirit
Tears others down without seeing their unmet needs	Builds others up according to their inner needs

"Do not let any unwholesome talk come out of your mouths, but only what is helpful for building others up according to their needs, that it may benefit those who listen" (Ephesians 4:29).

A Critical Spirit	A Caring Spirit
Publicly criticizes those who have wronged them without first going to them	Privately confronts those who have wronged them—by first going to them

"If your brother or sister sins, go and point out their fault, just between the two of you. If they listen to you, you have won them over" (Matthew 18:15).

A Critical Spirit	A Caring Spirit
Reacts pridefully when given advice	Responds positively when given advice

"Where there is strife, there is pride, but wisdom is found in those who take advice" (Proverbs 13:10).

A Critical Spirit	A Caring Spirit
Lacks mercy toward others	Extends mercy toward others

"Speak and act as those who are going to be judged by the law that gives freedom, because judgment without mercy will be shown to anyone who has not been merciful. Mercy triumphs over judgment" (James 2:12–13).

> The old saying is true:
> "People don't *care* how much you *know*
> until they *know* how much you *care*."

Honor Your Father and Mother

QUESTION: "I want to be biblical, but how can I honor my mother who has a critical spirit and is verbally abusive toward me?"

ANSWER: Submitting to your mother's abuse is not honoring her, but is dishonoring to her because you are enabling her to continue a sinful habit. When you love someone, you want to do what is best for them.

You can honor your mother by ...

▶ Living a godly life that reflects positively on her.

▶ Not assuming false guilt when blamed for situations in which you are blameless.

▶ Becoming emotionally and spiritually healthy, which will mean setting healthy boundaries for your relationship. You could say something similar to this ...

- "Mother, I genuinely care about you and love you. Right now I have a concern—if you speak negatively to me or about others, it reflects negatively on you."

23

- "Therefore, it's not in *your* best interest to continue with negative comments, and it's not in *my* best interest to continue to hear the negative criticism."

- "From now on, every time you speak with harsh criticism, I'm going to leave for a short time. I'll be back, but leaving will help me to have a more positive attitude."

- "I want to honor you by expecting the best of you. I know we are capable of better and healthier ways of communicating, and I want us to have the best relationship possible."

With this caring spirit, you can adhere to God's command to ...

"Honor your father and your mother."
(Exodus 20:12)

Job is called *blameless* by God, but he's not a *sinless* man. Blamelessness signifies a lifestyle characterized by righteousness, but it doesn't mean that perfection has been achieved. In fact, Job's spiraling despair turns his focus to God, who is silent but not absent, and soon accusations loom large in the man once called blameless. Rather than searching his soul to pursue greater righteousness, Job raises a "smoke screen" and begins to accuse God of injustice.

> **"I say to God: Do not declare me guilty, but tell me what charges you have against me. ...**
> **Are your days like those of a mortal or your years like those of a strong man,**
> **that you must search out my faults and probe after my sin—though you know that I am not guilty and that no one can rescue me from your hand?"**
> **(Job 10:2, 5–7)**

Some criminals use *smoke screens* when they commit crimes. Setting off a smoke bomb serves as a camouflage—a diversion and a covering for illegal behavior. Smoke screens are specifically designed to obscure, confuse, and mislead others.

Can you think of a time when you used a smoke screen to divert attention away from your own flaws —hiding your wrongs behind a "wall of smoke"? Having a critical spirit not only draws attention away from your own faults, but also focuses attention on the faults of others in an attempt to increase your sense of self-worth.

For example, if you are harboring *bitterness*, you might blame others for your bitter spirit. If you are *envious* of what others have, you could be critical of their success. These are both classic smoke screens. But look at what the Bible says ...

> **"If you harbor bitter envy
> and selfish ambition in your hearts,
> do not boast about it or deny the truth."
> (James 3:14)**

The Smoke Screen

A critical spirit is evident based on a combination of classic characteristics that critical people exhibit. The following list will help you recognize and better understand those who have a critical spirit. In addition, you can use it as a personal test to gain insight into your own smoke screens.

S—**SPREADING** harmful gossip with the justification that "everyone ought to know"

M—**MAKING** others feel embarrassed about their success while secretly envying them

O—**OBJECTING** to criticism from others to avoid personal accountability

K—**KIDDING** someone with the intent to hurt

E—**ENGAGING** in "constructive criticism" when the criticism is in no way constructive

S—SHIFTING blame to someone else when you yourself are to blame

C—CRITICIZING someone's happiness because you are unhappy

R—REMINDING others of their past failures to avoid attracting attention to your failures

E—EMPLOYING sarcastic humor as a weapon to attack

E—ELEVATING yourself by putting others down

N—NURTURING perfectionistic tendencies to make yourself look better

What a picture Jesus paints of the *faultfinder*! Imagine a beam of wood embedded in your eye. It's too large for you to dislodge without immense pain. It's too terrifying to think of other people prying it out. The solution seems simple: Ignore it, deny it, and create a smoke screen so no one will notice it.

But you can't hide the beam from the Lord's view. That's why in the Gospel of Luke, Jesus says: *"How can you say to your brother, 'Brother, let me take the speck out of your eye,' when you yourself fail to see the plank in your own eye? You hypocrite, first take the plank out of your eye, and then you will see clearly to remove the speck from you brother's eye"* (Luke 6:42).

A Wife's Faultfinding Friends

QUESTION: "What can I say to friends who bad-mouth my husband? The things they say about him keep me focused on his faults."

ANSWER: Set boundaries with your friends as to what you *will* and *will not* listen to in regard to your husband.

▶ **Explain** that you have determined to switch your focus from your husband's faults to his needs and to pray that your husband would let the Lord meet his deepest inner needs.

▶ **Elicit** their help—ask them to help you dwell on his positive traits. If your friends continue to be negative, they are not real friends, and you may need to limit your time with them.

▶ **Express** your concern with a pleasant voice: "I realize what you are saying is true but I cannot change him; only God can do that."

▶ **Emphasize** your course of action: "I am choosing to thank God that (mention a positive quality: he is a good provider or he is good to the children). Help me focus on his positive traits and pray that he will allow God to correct his faults, which is what God's Word tells me to do."

> "Above all, love each other deeply,
> because love covers over
> a multitude of sins."
> (1 Peter 4:8)

Zo (Zophar) is tired of sitting on the sidelines. He wants to demonstrate his "superior" understanding of God's ways before Job. With a harsher tone than the other two friends and through the use of put-downs and slander, Zo wants to silence Job once and for all, hoping he'll finally admit that gross sins have brought great tragedy to his life: *"Are all these words to go unanswered? Is this talker to be vindicated? Will your idle talk reduce others to silence? Will no one rebuke you when you mock?"* (Job 11:2–3).

And then slipping into vicious sarcasm, Zo insinuates that Job is witless and that he has as much of a chance to become wise as a donkey has of giving birth to a person.

> **"But the witless can no more become**
> **wise than a wild donkey's colt**
> **can be born human."**
> **(Job 11:12)**

Most people who display a critical spirit appear *strong* to the average observer because of the boldness with which they spew out their critical comments. In truth, criticism is more often the weapon of the *weak* than of the strong. It serves both to disguise their perceived inner deficiencies and to deceive others into thinking they are self-assured and confident.

Yet the Bible says ...

**"Blessed is the one whose sin the Lord
does not count against them
and in whose spirit is no deceit."
(Psalm 32:2)**

People who possess a critical spirit have certain characteristics that are camouflaged—not evident to most people. These camouflaged characteristics include ...

C—**CONCEALING** personal hurts and hopes out of distrust and fear of being abandoned

A—**ALLOWING** no one to get close enough to know the "real" person because of a fear of being rejected and scorned

M—**MANIPULATING** others into feeling guilty when they are not in an effort to conceal their own guilt

O—**OBTAINING** revenge for personal offenses in order to even the score and feel a sense of power, control, and self-respect

U—**USING** put-downs and slander to hurt others in an attempt to feel superior and significant

F—**FEELING** they are better than others to increase self-esteem and diminish feelings of inferiority

L—**LEVERAGING** to be "one up" on others to establish a position of control and to compensate for feeling vulnerable, like a victim

A—**ASSUMING** they are always right because being wrong is totally demeaning and demoralizing

G—**GIVING** little or no thought to the needs of others as a result of expending too much mental and emotional energy on meeting personal needs

E—**ENJOYING** few pleasures in life because the pressing need to be hypervigilant robs them of life's enjoyments

Those who attempt to conceal these classic characteristics constantly hide the truth from themselves and others. Unable to meet an unattainable standard, they pull others down to their perceived level, but all in vain. They may succeed in hiding the truth from themselves and others, but they can never hide from God. He not only sees their sin, He also knows their need.

> **"You, God, know my folly;**
> **my guilt is not hidden from you."**
> **(Psalm 69:5)**

CAUSES FOR A CRITICAL SPIRIT

In exhibiting their critical spirits, Job's three friends seem to be struggling for a sense of superiority and a desire to be proven right in their allegation that Job is indeed a sinner who is a victim of God's disciplinary hand. Realize, at one time Job was labeled *"the greatest man among all the people of the East"* (Job 1:3). Although still holding on to his integrity, Job knows his status now has hit rock bottom.

> **"I have become a laughingstock to my friends, though I called on God and he answered—a mere laughingstock, though righteous and blameless!"**
> **(Job 12:4)**

Why are some people so judgmental? A critical spirit doesn't appear out of nowhere—it is created and nurtured by past negative experiences. Don't just focus on the present problem. Instead, look back to the past. What could have produced the critical spirit and what continues to perpetuate it? Scripture points to the source of contentious behavior.

> **"What causes fights and quarrels among you? Don't they come from your desires that battle within you?"**
> **(James 4:1)**

What was life like for Eli, Bill, and Zo growing up? Were they nurtured in a positive environment, or did caustic words of criticism cloud their days?

We don't know for sure, yet it's curious that none of the three friends rises to Job's defense in the midst of this verbal bombardment. In fact, they seem to feed off of each other as they hammer an already crushed spirit.

But the call of God's Word is to ...

**"Defend the weak and the fatherless; uphold
the cause of the poor
and the oppressed.
Rescue the weak and the needy;
deliver them from the hand of the wicked."
(Psalm 82:3–4)**

The most common cause of a critical spirit is living in a home where criticism abounds—where parents model a critical spirit before their children. Growing up in such a home where critical comments are continually hurled can cause a child to be overly critical in adulthood. After all, with children, more is *caught* than *taught*.

Overly critical parents produce heavyhearted children. They feel continually crushed by criticism. Thus, their sense of self-worth is suffocated; they feel stuck in self-defeat.

Ultimately, condemning parents can provoke their children to anger—children who, under the weight of such pressure become "stone throwers." The book of Proverbs presents a poignant word picture of the damaging weight produced by judgmental people who provoke others to feel or act negatively.

"Stone is heavy and sand a burden, but a fool's provocation is heavier than both." (Proverbs 27:3)

A critical spirit is developed under the weight of:

▶ Unanticipated anger	▶ Ungrounded guilt
▶ Unremitting stress	▶ Unjust rejection
▶ Undue pressure	▶ Unmerited blame
▶ Unending fear	▶ Unreasonable control
▶ Unfair comparison	▶ Unwarranted attacks
▶ Undeserved condemnation	▶ Unsubstantiated accusation

Typically, those who live under the pressure of continual criticism feel the excess weight of false guilt. In truth, they could have easily written these words ...

"My guilt has overwhelmed me like a burden too heavy to bear." (Psalm 38:4)

Job has discovered for himself that there is no bigger lie than the old childhood adage: "Sticks and stones may break my bones but words will never hurt me." This saying could not be further from the truth.

The accusing words of Eli, Bill, and Zo deliver blow after blow to Job's spirit. They relentlessly accuse Job of being a sinner and associate shame with his contemptible condition. Zo misguidedly assures ...

"If you put away the sin that is in your hand and allow no evil to dwell in your tent, then, free of fault, you will lift up your face; you will stand firm and without fear."
(Job 11:14–15)

It's true: "Sticks and stones may break my bones..." However, when faultfinding words are wrong, the same saying can have a vastly different ending: "...but words can break my heart." Critical comments can cause extensive, even lifetime, harm. No visible wounds will show, but the damage to the spirit of a child can be devastating.

Many children who are assaulted with wounding words resort to criticism as a means of self-defense. To try to lessen the impact of their own emotional pain, *they stay on the attack.*

When painful words are played over and over in children's minds, they may retaliate. This explains why so many "hurt people ... *hurt people*!" Children who are raised in an overly critical home experience great emotional pain.

> **"I am poor and needy, and my heart is wounded within me." (Psalm 109:22)**

Emotionally hurt children feel the pain of ...

H—**HARSHNESS**; communicating, "You're not worth any kindness."

U—**UNCONCERN**; communicating, "You have no value."

R—**REJECTION**; communicating, "You're not acceptable."

T—**TAUNTING**; communicating, "You deserve to be insulted."

A critical spirit starts out as a defense tactic. Typically, if one child hits another, the second hits back. Striking back when attacked is a natural defensive response—a natural protection. When you are in a position of having little power, you are unable to protect yourself from the attacks of someone who has much power.

Consequently, you can become skilled in verbal attacks as a means of defense. However, if you want to be blessed with positive relationships, staying on the attack will never solve the problem. That is why the Bible says, *"Do not repay evil with evil or insult with insult. On the contrary, repay evil with blessing, because to this you were called so that you may inherit a blessing"* (1 Peter 3:9).

Job has had enough and hopes to quiet his "friends-turned-accusers" once and for all. *"You, however, smear me with lies; you are worthless physicians, all of you! If only you would be altogether silent! For you, that would be wisdom"* (Job 13:4–5). But the cycle of criticism continues. All three accusers keep up the verbal pounding, which prompts this battered man to plead before his God …

"Only grant me these two things, God, and then I will not hide from you: Withdraw your hand far from me, and stop frightening me with your terrors." (Job 13:20–21)

The painful situations we experience as children are processed by our soul—our mind, will, and emotions. Over time, we can develop a negative pattern of reacting to these painful situations (becoming critical), a pattern that can remain with us into and throughout our adulthood. We must rely on the transforming work of the Holy Spirit within us to help us overcome a critical spirit.

When you are trapped in a cycle of critical thinking you may exclaim, "I can't help reacting this way!" Yet your emotions are merely *responding* to what your mind thinks. Therefore, the cycle is this: Your negative thoughts produce your negative emotions, which, in turn, produce your negative actions.

Since the cycle of criticism begins in our thoughts, we need to heed what the Bible tells us about renewing our minds and appropriate the mind of Christ. With God's help we can change our thoughts and then experience a changed life. Scripture says it this way: *"Do not conform to the pattern of this world, but be transformed by the renewing of your mind"* (Romans 12:2).

Whenever a negative situation occurs in your life, you have a choice as to *how you think* about it—which determines *how you respond*. Children often develop patterns of thinking that dictate their feelings and ultimately their actions. The natural progression occurs as follows:

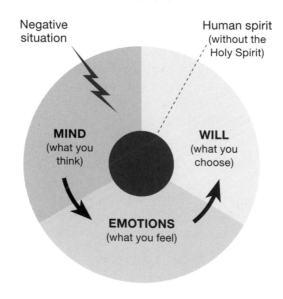

YOUR SOUL
Self-Directed Reaction
Mind → Emotions → Will

Negative situation

Human spirit (without the Holy Spirit)

MIND (what you think)

WILL (what you choose)

EMOTIONS (what you feel)

EXAMPLE #1

Negative Situation: Someone verbally cuts you down.

NATURAL HUMAN RESPONSE

▶ **Your mind** records the cruel words and thinks angry *thoughts*. ("He's so hateful.") Many children develop a critical spirit because of the way they process the pain in their lives, and this process is naturally influenced by the ways the significant people in their lives have processed their own pain. (Children often do what was modeled before them.)

▶ **Your emotions** respond with angry *feelings*. ("I hate him.") Because children are not physically or emotionally mature enough to analyze their thinking process, they base their decisions more on emotions than on reasoning. By the time children have developed their capacity for analysis and reasoning, their patterns of reacting are already established.

▶ **Your will** reacts with angry *behavior*. (You act in hateful ways.) Responding in kind with nasty, verbal attacks or angry, argumentative shouting is a natural human response that follows angry thoughts and angry feelings. This type of response only continues cycles of behavior that destroy rather than give life. As Paul described, *"Those who live according to the flesh have their minds set on what the flesh desires. ... The mind governed by the flesh is death"* (Romans 8:5–6).

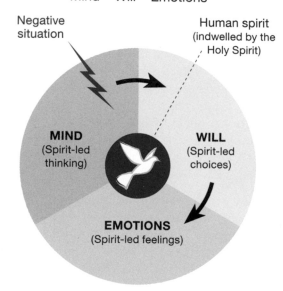

YOUR SOUL
Spirit-Directed Reaction
Mind → Will → Emotions

Negative situation

Human spirit (indwelled by the Holy Spirit)

MIND
(Spirit-led thinking)

WILL
(Spirit-led choices)

EMOTIONS
(Spirit-led feelings)

EXAMPLE #2

Negative Situation: Someone verbally cuts you down.

SPIRIT-LED RESPONSE

▶ **Your mind** records the unjust words, and the Holy Spirit, as your Counselor, *teaches your mind* how to think about the offense.

"The Counselor, the Holy Spirit—the Father will send Him in My name—will teach you all things and remind you of everything I have told you" (John 14:26 HCSB).

"His words were so hateful. But there must be something painfully broken in his life. I will do what the Bible tells me to do—I need to *'pray for those who persecute* [me].'" (Read Matthew 5:44.)

▶ **Your will** acts with prayer as the Spirit *directs your will* toward the right choice. As your Conscience, He convicts you to pray, whether you feel like it or not.

"When he, the Spirit of truth, comes, he will guide you into all the truth. He will not speak on his own; he will speak only what he hears, and he will tell you what is yet to come" (John 16:13).

"Lord, I pray that (name of critic) will allow You to meet the need for healing whatever past pain is still causing (name of critic) problems."

▶ **Your emotions** respond with compassion as the Spirit *controls your emotions.*

"Hope does not put us to shame, because God's love has been poured out into our hearts through the Holy Spirit, who has been given to us" (Romans 5:5).

As you pray, the Comforter evokes from you loving compassion toward the unjust person who is spiritually needy.

" ... those who live in accordance with the Spirit have their minds set on what the Spirit desires. ... the mind governed by the Spirit is life and peace."
(Romans 8:5–6)

As Job is berated by his accusatory companions, he begins to develop a critical spirit toward God that borders on blasphemy. He accuses God of denying him justice and makes a daring proclamation: *"Oh, that I had someone to hear me! I sign now my defense—let the Almighty answer me; let my accuser put his indictment in writing. Surely I would wear it on my shoulder, I would put it on like a crown. I would give him an account of my every step; I would present it to him as to a ruler"* (Job 31:35–37). Self-centeredness and self-righteousness have surfaced in this man of God.

The Bible warns and proclaims ...

> **"If we claim to be without sin, we deceive ourselves and the truth is not in us.
> If we confess our sins, he is faithful and just and will forgive us our sins and purify us from all unrighteousness."**
> **(1 John 1:8–9)**

In essence, the sin committed by Adam and Eve in the Garden of Eden was self-centeredness—the desire for self-sufficiency and self-will apart from God's will, the desire to take on God's role and to be in total control. Self-will and desire for control has been passed on to everyone in the human family.

This inherent sin nature in unbelievers and the residual sinful patterns in believers cause those with a critical spirit to see others as inferior and in need of knowing when they are at fault. This is the essence of a critical spirit: assuming a superior role of faultfinding with a derogatory view of others.

In the Garden of Eden, God asked Adam to give an account of himself. Although Adam knew he had sinned, he first blamed God for giving him Eve, then blamed Eve for giving him the infamous forbidden fruit.

> **"The man said, 'The woman you put here with me—she gave me some fruit from the tree, and I ate it.'"**
> **(Genesis 3:12)**

Adam was the first, but certainly not the last to shift blame to God—and then to someone else—rather than taking personal responsibility for his own wrong choice.

For some with a critical spirit, putting others down creates a false sense of significance—a sense of power, a sense of pride—at least temporarily. For them the Bible warns ...

> **"When pride comes, then comes disgrace, but with humility comes wisdom."**
> **(Proverbs 11:2)**

Three God-Given Inner Needs

In reality, we have all been created with three God-given inner needs: the needs for love, significance, and security.[6]

▶ **Love**—to know that someone is unconditionally committed to our best interest

"My command is this: Love each other as I have loved you" (John 15:12).

▶ **Significance**—to know that our lives have meaning and purpose

"I cry out to God Most High, to God who fulfills his purpose for me" (Psalm 57:2 ESV).

▶ **Security**—to feel accepted and a sense of belonging

"Whoever fears the LORD has a secure fortress, and for their children it will be a refuge" (Proverbs 14:26).

The Ultimate Need-Meeter

Why did God give us these deep inner needs, knowing that people and self-effort fail us?

God gave us these inner needs so that we would come to know Him as our Need-Meeter. Our needs are designed by God to draw us into a deeper dependence on Christ. God did not create any person or position or any amount of power or possessions to meet the deepest needs in our lives. If a person or thing *could* meet all our needs, we wouldn't need God! The Lord will use circumstances and bring positive people into our lives as an extension of His care and compassion, but ultimately only God can satisfy all the needs of our hearts.

The Bible says ...

> **"The Lord will guide you always;**
> **he will satisfy your needs in a sun-scorched**
> **land and will strengthen your frame.**
> **You will be like a well-watered garden,**
> **like a spring whose waters never fail."**
> **(Isaiah 58:11)**

The apostle Paul revealed this truth by first asking, *"What a wretched man I am! Who will rescue me from this body that is subject to death?"* He then answers his own question by saying he is rescued by *"Jesus Christ our Lord!"* (Romans 7:24–25).

All along, the Lord planned to meet our deepest needs for ...

▶ **Love**—*"I* [the Lord] *have loved you with an everlasting love; I have drawn you with unfailing kindness"* (Jeremiah 31:3).

▶ **Significance**—*"'For I know the plans I have for you,' declares the Lord, 'plans to prosper you and not to harm you, plans to give you hope and a future'"* (Jeremiah 29:11).

▶ **Security**—*"The Lord himself goes before you and will be with you; he will never leave you nor forsake you. Do not be afraid; do not be discouraged"* (Deuteronomy 31:8).

The truth is that our God-given needs for love, significance, and security can be legitimately met in Christ Jesus! Philippians 4:19 makes it plain ...

"My God will meet all your needs according to the riches of his glory in Christ Jesus."

▶ Wrong Belief

"My sense of significance is increased when I point out the wrongs of others. The fact that I believe 'I am right' justifies my criticism of others."

But the Bible says, *"You, therefore, have no excuse, you who pass judgment on someone else, for at whatever point you judge another, you are condemning yourself, because you who pass judgment do the same things"* (Romans 2:1).

Right Belief

"When I am critical of others, I am actually exposing my own sin. Because Christ lives in me, continually extending His mercy toward me, I will reflect His compassion by caring about the needs of others rather than by criticizing them."

The Bible says, *"... encourage the disheartened, help the weak, be patient with everyone. Make sure that nobody pays back wrong for wrong, but always strive to do what is good for each other and for everyone else"* (1 Thessalonians 5:14–15).

HOW CAN You Escape Criticism throughout Eternity?

In the midst of suffering, Job seems to sway between what he *knows* about God and what he *feels* about Him. Job knows that God isn't unjust, but it feels like He's unjust. The book of Job is renowned for a mighty proclamation of faith that has inspired strugglers all around the world. Here, Job expresses what he knows about God ...

**"I know that my redeemer lives, and that in the end he will stand on the earth. And after my skin has been destroyed, yet in my flesh I will see God; I myself will see him with my own eyes—I, and not another. How my heart yearns within me!"
(Job 19:25–27)**

If you're in despair from critical, caustic words, there is Someone right now who is eagerly waiting to have a relationship with you. God is inviting you into His family, and be assured, you'll never hear a single critical word in the heavenly home that awaits. God wants to bring you hope and healing, and He wants to save you from eternal condemnation.

When you enter into a right relationship with God, you are spiritually adopted into the family of God and will always be loved, esteemed, and honored. The Bible says ...

"There is now no condemnation for those who are in Christ Jesus." (Romans 8:1)

Scripture gives us four spiritual truths for beginning a relationship with God. He has graciously provided a way to bridge the spiritual gap that separates Him from us.

The Four Points of God's Plan

#1 God's Purpose for You is *Salvation*.

What was God's motivation in sending Jesus Christ to earth?

To express His love for you by saving you!

The Bible says, *"God so loved the world that he gave his one and only Son, that whoever believes in him shall not perish but have eternal life. For God did not send his Son into the world to condemn the world, but to save the world through him"* (John 3:16–17).

What was Jesus' purpose in coming to earth?

To forgive your sins, to empower you to have victory over sin, and to enable you to live a fulfilled life!

Jesus said, *"I have come that they may have life, and that they may have it more abundantly"* (John 10:10 NKJV).

#2 Your Problem is *Sin*.

What exactly is sin?

Sin is living independently of God's standard—knowing what is right, but choosing what is wrong.

The Bible says, *"If anyone, then, knows the good they ought to do and doesn't do it, it is sin for them"* (James 4:17).

What is the major consequence of sin?

Spiritual death, eternal separation from God.

Scripture states, *"Your iniquities* [sins] *have separated you from your God"* (Isaiah 59:2).

"The wages of sin is death, but the gift of God is eternal life in Christ Jesus our Lord" (Romans 6:23).

#3 God's Provision for You is the *Savior.*

Can anything remove the penalty for sin?

Yes! Jesus died on the cross to personally pay the penalty for your sins.

The Bible says, *"God demonstrates his own love for us in this: While we were still sinners, Christ died for us"* (Romans 5:8).

What is the solution to being separated from God?

Belief in (entrusting your life to) Jesus Christ as the only way to God the Father.

Jesus says, *"I am the way and the truth and the life. No one comes to the Father except through me"* (John 14:6).

"Believe in the Lord Jesus, and you will be saved" (Acts 16:31).

#4 Your Part is *Surrender.*

Give Christ control of your life, entrusting yourself to Him.

"Jesus said to his disciples, 'Whoever wants to be my disciple must deny themselves and take up their cross [die to your own self-rule] *and follow me. For whoever wants to save their life will lose it, but whoever loses their life for me will find it. What good will it be for someone to gain the whole world, yet forfeit their soul?'"* (Matthew 16:24–26).

Place your faith in (rely on) Jesus Christ as your personal Lord and Savior and reject your "good works" as a means of earning God's approval.

"It is by grace you have been saved, through faith—and this is not from yourselves, it is the gift of God—not by works, so that no one can boast" (Ephesians 2:8–9).

The moment you choose to receive Jesus as your Lord and Savior—entrusting your life to Him—He comes to live inside you. Then He gives you His power to live the fulfilled life God has planned for you.

If you want to be fully forgiven by God and become the person God created you to be, you can tell Him in a simple, heartfelt prayer like this:

PRAYER OF SALVATION

*"God, I want a real relationship with You.
I admit that many times I've chosen to go
my own way instead of Your way.
Please forgive me for my sins.
Jesus, thank You for dying on the cross to
pay the penalty for my sins.
Come into my life to be my Lord
and my Savior.
Change me from the inside out
and make me the person
You created me to be.
In Your holy name I pray. Amen."*

WHAT CAN YOU NOW EXPECT?

If you sincerely prayed this prayer, look at what God says about you!

**"Very truly I tell you, whoever hears my word
and believes him who sent me
has eternal life and will not be judged
but has crossed over from death to life."
(John 5:24)**

STEPS TO SOLUTION

The Lord is using traumatic trials to help Job gain a greater understanding of God and to grow Job into a more faith-filled man of God. Ultimately, the Lord is Job's "heavenly sandpaper." And no matter how tough Job's tragedies, they will not take his life. In fact, honor—double honor—is just around the corner. For the Bible says, *"whoever heeds correction is honored"* (Proverbs 13:18).

Like Job, we all need a little "heavenly sandpaper" to help smooth over the "rough edges." But those who appoint themselves to be our personal heavenly sandpaper can leave us worn down, emotionally rubbed raw. Without a doubt, God uses our close relationships to teach us the truth about ourselves—the truth about our rough edges. But rather than wearing us down, He builds us up so that we can become all He created us to be. Rather than leaving us discouraged, He helps us feel encouraged and causes us to change.

Clearly, *constructive criticism* can reveal specific areas in our lives that need to be refined. But when you seek to give "constructive" criticism, be certain that God has directed your words—that they are carefully chosen and spoken in truth and with love. But be aware, too much coarse sanding will be resented and result in being rejected. Prideful criticism will always be rejected.

However, if the criticism of you is incorrect, be calm—not curt or critical. The book of Proverbs makes this point plain: *"A fool's mouth lashes out with pride, but the lips of the wise protect them"* (Proverbs 14:3).

Key Verse to Memorize

Job's three finger-pointing friends speak words that are terribly distasteful—words too difficult to stomach. Rather than their conversation being filled with grace, they are filled with faultfinding. The unholy trio is determined to get Job to own up to his supposed guilt, while Job is just as determined to maintain his innocence.

This negative approach does nothing to encourage positive relationships. People get stuck in a stalemate—and no one wins. So whether you give or receive constructive criticism, the Bible says ...

> *"Let your conversation be always full of grace, seasoned with salt, so that you may know how to answer everyone."*
> (Colossians 4:6)

Why salt? Known as "white gold" in ancient times, salt has always been highly valued. Previously used as money for commercial trade, today salt is used: (1) to *season* food, which enhances flavor, (2) to *clean* cuts and abrasions, which acts as a disinfectant, (3) to *melt* icy roads and sidewalks, which prevents different kinds of accidents, and (4) to *preserve* food, which without refrigeration keeps it from quickly spoiling.

When the Bible says, *"Let your conversation be ... seasoned with salt."* Envision the "salt" of your words being used wisely ...

▶ **To produce** enhanced enjoyment in all of your relationships

▶ **To purify** your wounded relationships by speaking healing, grace-filled words

▶ **To prevent** the accidental "slip of the tongue" and the use of caustic, critical words

▶ **To preserve** your reputation and keep it from being spoiled

Scripture reminds us ...

"You are the salt of the earth. But if the salt loses its saltiness, how can it be made salty again? It is no longer good for anything, except to be thrown out and trampled underfoot." (Matthew 5:13)

Key Passage to Read

JAMES 3:1–12

Job feels the piercing power of the tongue unleashed by his three friends. But another man stands waiting in the wings for a chance to speak—to use his own tongue in an attempt to impart truth.

Elihu—let's call him Hugh—the youngest of Job's visitors is angry with all of them. None of Job's friends finds a way to refute him, yet they all find ways to condemn him. And he's upset at Job's implication that God would be unjust.

Oh, the power of the tongue! Isn't it interesting how small objects can possess great power? The power of the *tongue* seems far out of proportion to its size. A large horse is controlled by a small bit in its mouth, and an enormous ship is controlled by a small rudder. James 3:5 says ...

"Likewise, the tongue is a small part of the body, but it makes great boasts. Consider what a great forest is set on fire by a small spark."

We can learn much from James 3:3–12. The tongue, though little, can be ...

▶ **Powerful** like a small bit, turning a huge horse (v. 3).

▶ **Forceful** like a small rudder, steering a massive ship (v. 4).

▶ **Dangerous** like a tiny spark, igniting a great forest fire (v. 5).

▶ **Devastating** like a searing fire, burning the whole body (v. 6).

▶ **Corrupting** like an evil force, instigated by hell (v. 6).

▶ **Untameable** like a restless evil, full of deadly poison (v. 8).

▶ **Contaminating** like a two-faced hypocrite, both praising and cursing others (v. 10).

▶ **Distasteful** like a flowing spring, embittered by salt water (v. 11).

▶ **Contradictory** like a fig tree bearing olives — like a grapevine bearing figs (v. 12).

Based on the Bible, this fact is true: Polluted water and pure water cannot pour out of the same stream. Likewise, if praise to God and criticism of others flow from the same mouth, the conflicting inconsistencies reveal that something is desperately wrong with the source—the heart is impure, for Luke 6:45 (ESV) reveals, *"out of the abundance of the heart"* the mouth speaks.

HOW TO Stop Growing a Crop of Criticism

Hugh starts out with the voice of reason amidst a torrent of emotion. *"So listen to me, you men of understanding. Far be it from God to do evil, from the Almighty to do wrong. ... It is unthinkable that God would do wrong, that the Almighty would pervert justice"* (Job 34:10, 12).

While Hugh eloquently espouses truths about the character of God, he—like the others—eventually grows a crop of criticism where Job is concerned. He wrongly assesses the cause of Job's multiple tragedies.

"Is there anyone like Job, who drinks scorn like water? He keeps company with evildoers; he associates with the wicked" (Job 34:7–8). Hugh pressures Job to repent and proclaims: *"Now you are laden with the judgment due the wicked; judgment and justice have taken hold of you"* (Job 36:17).

But the criticism will stop when God speaks. And, oh, will He speak!

In truth, you can grow a "crop of criticism" even if you usually are not a critical person. These "crops" can suddenly sprout up through circumstances in which you cast a critical eye or bend a critical ear. With the source of your criticism rooted in resentment toward others, you eagerly point out their flaws. You may not recognize when you are being overly critical, but God does, and so do those who know you best.

The Bible even says ...

"All a person's ways seem pure to them, but motives are weighed by the LORD." (Proverbs 16:2)

If you desire to quit growing a crop of criticism, first pray that you will see your "seeds" of criticism from God's perspective. Then ask yourself:

▶ **What kind of looks** do I give when I'm being critical?

▶ **How do I act** when I'm being critical?

▶ **Do I express** a critical attitude ...

- When I'm around certain people (family, friends, coworkers, acquaintances, neighbors)? Who: _____

- When I'm required to go to unpleasant places? Where: _____

- When I must engage in undesirable activities (social, work, recreational)? What: _____

- When I feel unsettling sensations (anger, fear, frustration, grief, embarrassment, disgust, impatience)? Which one(s): _____

- When I have been unjustly treated (disrespected, ignored, misquoted, insulted)? How: _____

- When I think about those who are unlike me (educationally, physically, socially, racially, politically, spiritually)? Who: _____

- When I talk about controversial issues (political, religious, moral, or personal convictions)? Which one(s): _____

▶ **Why do I have a critical spirit** toward these people, places, or situations?

(Explore the reasons for each one listed.)

Once you have identified your crop of criticism, pray for God's discernment to:

▶ **Explain** your crops of criticism to someone spiritually mature who is able to support you in making godly changes.

▶ **Enlist** the help of an accountability partner in making two lists: first, those whom you need to forgive and second, those from whom you need to ask forgiveness.

▶ **Exercise** your resolve to ask forgiveness of others and to extend forgiveness to others.

▶ **Examine** your thought life in light of God's Word.

▶ **Enter** into an agreement with God to allow His Word to "sift out" your critical spirit.

▶ **Expel** all thoughts that do not pass through God's scriptural grid.

▶ **Exchange** your critical thinking for God's correct thinking.

"Whatever is true, whatever is noble, whatever is right, whatever is pure, whatever is lovely, whatever is admirable— if anything is excellent or praiseworthy— think about such things." (Philippians 4:8)

HOW TO Change a Critical Heart into a Caring Heart

Suppose someone said to you, "When I think of you, I think of Jesus." How would you feel? In the deepest part of your heart, wouldn't you like to have the character of Christ be evident in your life? If so, what was He really like?

Do you perceive Jesus as having a critical spirit or a caring spirit? Did Jesus have a judgmental spirit toward people, or did the truth He spoke judge them? And when His words exposed the sinful reality of their hearts, were they not accompanied by a merciful offer of redemption?

People were drawn to Jesus because He was an encourager, not a critic. While He didn't ignore sinful behavior, He wasn't the classic "faultfinder" either. Instead, He was concerned with recognizing and meeting needs, most importantly our need to have our sins forgiven through His death and resurrection.

When you experience authentic salvation, the Bible says you have *"Christ in you"* (Colossians 1:27); therefore, you have the capacity to care rather than to criticize. If you truly want to be like Christ, don't be a critic—enlarge your heart to become an encourager.[7]

"If you have any encouragement from being united with Christ, if any comfort from his love, if any common sharing in the Spirit, if any tenderness and compassion, then make my joy complete by being like-minded, having the same love, being one in spirit and of one mind."
(Philippians 2:1–2)

▶ **A caring heart sees** its own shortcomings.

- Humble your heart to see your own sin, your imperfections, and your immense need for God's mercy.

- Rather than measuring yourself by human standards, measure yourself by God's standard—the perfect Savior.

- Instead of making sure others see how significant you are, help them see *their* significance in God's eyes.

- Pray, "Lord, may I see my sin as You see it, and may I hate my sin as You hate it."

"Search me, God, and know my heart; test me and know my anxious thoughts. See if there is any offensive way in me, and lead me in the way everlasting" (Psalm 139:23–24).

▶ **A caring heart has** active compassion for others.

- Look closely at the life of Christ to learn His compassionate way of confronting the truth.

- Consider the woman caught in adultery—a crime in that day worthy of death. Jesus didn't focus on her fault. Instead of condemning her, He looked beyond her fault and saw her need. Then He compassionately met that need. (Read John 8:3–11.)

- Look at the woman at the well who had been in multiple marriages and was living with yet another man. Although Jesus knew all about her, He didn't focus on her fault. Without ignoring her sin, He chose to focus on her need and then compassionately met her need. (Read John 4:5–42.)

- Pray that you will not be a critical stone-thrower, but a compassionate "need-meeter."

"As God's chosen people, holy and dearly loved, clothe yourselves with compassion, kindness, humility, gentleness and patience" (Colossians 3:12).

▶ **A caring heart draws** out the heartfelt needs of others.

- Listen not only to what people say on the surface, but also for feelings beneath the surface—feelings of being unloved, insignificant, and insecure.

- Learn the "language of love" that speaks to the heart—a thoughtful note, a favorite food, a surprising gift, a tender touch, or reaching out to one of their loved ones.

- Ask: "What can I do to improve our relationship?" Listen carefully, then repeat what you hear.

  Reflect: "Are you saying _____? Is that what you said?"

  Clarify: "It sounds as if you feel _____"

  Explore: "I'm not sure I understand what you are saying."

  Extend: "Is there more? What else do you feel?"

  Offer: "What would be meaningful to you?"

- Pray that God will give you a discerning spirit as you seek to draw others out.

"The purposes of a person's heart are deep waters, but one who has insight draws them out" (Proverbs 20:5).

▶ **A caring heart offers** acceptance to others.

- Realize, everyone has an innate fear of rejection and a deep yearning for acceptance.

- Recognize, God accepts you just as you are, even with your faults. You are His beloved child in whom He takes much pleasure.

- Choose to be a channel through which God extends His acceptance to others.

- Pray for God to reveal the ways you have rejected others and the ways to reach out with a heart of acceptance.

"Accept the one whose faith is weak, without quarreling over disputable matters. ... for God has accepted them" (Romans 14:1, 3).

▶ **A caring heart sees** God-given worth in others.

- Recognize, the worth of something is most often demonstrated by the price paid for it.

- Look at how the Lord demonstrated the worth of every person by paying the highest price—His life. With His blood, He paid the necessary ransom to redeem you from the penalty of your sins.

- Treat every person—including the most problematic—as someone with God-given worth. After all, God judges our hearts, attitudes, and actions toward others.

- Pray that the Lord will not allow you to despise anyone He created. And pray that you will see others as God sees them, and value them as He values them.

"Are not five sparrows sold for two pennies? Yet not one of them is forgotten by God. Indeed, the very hairs of your head are all numbered. Don't be afraid; you are worth more than many sparrows" (Luke 12:6–7).

▶ **A caring heart praises** the positives in others.

- Refuse to be a pharisaical faultfinder. The Pharisees even found fault with the faultless Son of God.

- Avoid the temptation to "catch" people doing something wrong. Instead, comment on what they are doing right.

- Compliment outer characteristics (cleanliness, sweet countenance, modest clothing, etc.) and praise inner character: "I see that you have wisdom, perseverance, thoughtfulness, integrity."

- Pray that you will see something positive in every person, then faithfully make that your focus.

"The wisdom that comes from heaven is first of all pure; then peace-loving, considerate, submissive, full of mercy and good fruit, impartial and sincere" (James 3:17).

▶ **A caring heart doesn't wound** others with words.

- Understand the fallacy of the saying, "Talk is cheap." Talk is costly when it tears others down. Consider that what you are criticizing in someone may be something God wants to address directly with that person. Meanwhile, He wants you to remain silent and to pray.

- Before speaking words of criticism, ask a wise friend to evaluate your content and tone. Realize, after critical words are spoken, you can never take them back.

- Inspire those needing to change with your belief that they *can* change: "Don't give up. God will guide you in the way you should go. I know you can make the right decisions. I believe you can experience God's best."

- Pray for God to put His words into your mind and your mouth.

"Let the message of Christ dwell among you richly as you teach and admonish one another with all wisdom" (Colossians 3:16).

▶ **A caring heart sees** the unmet needs of others.

- Realize, people who put down others have at least one unmet inner need—the need for love, for significance, or for security.[8]

- Instead of judging the inappropriate actions of others, seek to understand the need behind their actions.

- Realize, people don't always mean what they say or even understand the needs behind what they say.

- Pray that your critics will allow the Lord to meet their deepest inner needs.

"My God will meet all your needs according to the riches of his glory in Christ Jesus" (Philippians 4:19).

▶ **A caring heart relies** on God's Word and God's Spirit for wisdom.

- Seek God's wisdom by reading a chapter a day from the book of Proverbs. This book of wisdom was written by Solomon, whom God gifted with supernatural wisdom. (Read 2 Chronicles 1:7–12.)

- Write down every verse from Proverbs that pertains to the tongue. By looking at this list, determine whether you are being wise with your words.

- See God at work in every circumstance and trust Him for wisdom to know how to respond. (Wisdom is the ability to look at life from God's point of view.)

- Pray for God's Spirit to teach you spiritual truths and lead you to speak these truths in love.

"This is what we speak, not in words taught us by human wisdom but in words taught by the Spirit, explaining spiritual realities with Spirit-taught words" (1 Corinthians 2:13).

When God finally confronts Job and his accusers, His constructive criticism of Job starts the process of personal transformation.

Job had flooded the heavens with questions about his desperately despondent situation. But God makes it clear—as Job's Creator—that now He'll be asking all the questions. The poignant truth is this: God owes us no answers.

The Lord also makes it clear that Job's accusations have cast a shadow over the character of God. Indeed, Job challenged God. In turn, God challenges Job!

> **"Then the LORD spoke to Job**
> **out of the storm. He said:**
> **'Who is this that obscures my plans with**
> **words without knowledge?**
> **Brace yourself like a man; I will question**
> **you, and you shall answer me.'"**
> **(Job 38:1–3)**

Being confronted about our personal wrong is never pleasant, but always necessary for spiritual growth and for developing healthy relationships. If you are to be conformed to the character of Christ, you must change. And change is the purpose of confrontation. God's heart for you is that you respond to confrontation with humility and wisdom, seeking God for keen discernment and the power to change when the criticism is legitimate. Change is never about pleasing people; it's about pleasing God, who commends those who heed constructive criticism.

"Whoever scorns instruction will pay for it, but whoever respects a command is rewarded." (Proverbs 13:13)

Resolve to respond to criticism in a way that is biblical and reflects the character of Christ.

▶ **Make** your relationship a priority over your need to always be right.

"The very fact that you have lawsuits among you means you have been completely defeated already. Why not rather be wronged? Why not rather be cheated?" (1 Corinthians 6:7).

▶ **Demonstrate** a heart willing to understand the other person's perspective. Be willing to change where necessary and to heal any relational tension.

"If it is possible, as far as it depends on you, live at peace with everyone" (Romans 12:18).

▶ **Listen** carefully, even if you disagree with the other person's opinion. Give yourself time to consider what the other person says before you respond.

"Everyone should be quick to listen, slow to speak and slow to become angry" (James 1:19).

▶ **Respond** with humility. Release your reputation to God and ask Him to help you with your relationships.

"Humble yourselves, therefore, under God's mighty hand, that he may lift you up in due time" (1 Peter 5:6).

▶ **Consider** those who confront you as being gifts from God. Flattery builds your pride, but confrontation helps you grow in the Lord.

"Wounds from a friend can be trusted, but an enemy multiplies kisses" (Proverbs 27:6).

▶ **Maintain** dignity and discernment. Allow God to speak to you through the other person. Your confronter may be someone who can help you overcome your critical attitudes. Even if you do not agree with your confronter, God may still use this opportunity for you to esteem the confronter for both the courage displayed in confronting you and for the value placed on your relationship.

"Those who disregard discipline despise themselves, but the one who heeds correction gains understanding" (Proverbs 15:32).

▶ **Consider** the counsel of your confronter without being defensive or reactive. God may be using this person to help you grow closer to Him. The benefits of confrontation may include coming closer to God, living a more loving lifestyle, and growing more intimate with your confronter.

"Whoever remains stiff-necked after many rebukes will suddenly be destroyed—without remedy" (Proverbs 29:1).

Job's self-righteousness and critical spirit are met by God Himself with a barrage of 72 questions, all intended to humble the man who tightly holds on to his integrity—the very man who questions God's integrity.

And several of the questions are laced with satire and irony, further revealing the personality of God. *"Where were you when I laid the earth's foundation? Tell me, if you understand. Who marked off its dimensions? Surely you know! ... What is the way to the abode of light? And where does darkness reside? Can you take them to their places? Do you know the paths to their dwellings? Surely you know, for you were already born! You have lived so many years!"* (Job 38:4–5, 19–21).

If you've had a critical spirit, you need to ask forgiveness from those you've criticized. In truth, you have a need to be forgiven, first by God and then by those you've criticized. However, asking for forgiveness can be difficult if you don't realize your need to be forgiven and the freedom it grants you.

Jesus makes it clear that *you are to go* to those you have offended before you approach God and even before you offer Him a gift at church!

In His own words ...

"If you are offering your gift at the altar and there remember that your brother or sister has something against you,

**leave your gift there in front of the altar.
First go and be reconciled to them;
then come and offer your gift."
(Matthew 5:23–24)**

If you have wounded people with your critical spirit, go to each one individually and ...

▶ **Acknowledge** your critical spirit.

"I realize I've been wrong. My critical spirit has been wrong toward you, and I am genuinely sorry."

▶ **Acknowledge** God's work in your life.

"God has clearly convicted me. He has been doing a work in my heart and has made me aware of how I have wronged you."

▶ **Acknowledge** your untrustworthiness.

"I realize you don't have any reason to trust me in this area right now because I haven't proven myself trustworthy. But I hope one day to prove that I can be trusted."

▶ **Ask** for clarification.

"You are important to me, and I can tell that I have wounded you. Would you please tell me in what other ways I may have hurt you? I genuinely want to know."

▶ **Ask** for further clarification.

"Are there other ways I have caused you pain?"

▶ **Acknowledge** each offense.

"I understand I have hurt you by _____."
For example, "I realize I have been insensitive
to you." (Using their words, mention every way
you have hurt them.)

▶ **Ask** forgiveness.

"I don't know whether you are willing to forgive
me right now, and I understand if you aren't. I
realize I don't deserve your forgiveness, but for
my hurtful actions toward you, I would like to
ask, 'Will you forgive me?'"

▶ **Acknowledge** your commitment.

"I am committed to allowing the Lord to continue
working in my heart and life to change me. I
thank you for helping me by having the courage
to be honest with me."

▶ **Acknowledge** your gratitude.

"I thank you for talking with me and allowing
me to apologize."

The Bible says to ...

> **"Be kind and compassionate
> to one another, forgiving each other,
> just as in Christ God forgave you."**
> **(Ephesians 4:32)**

As soon as God confronts Job for his critical spirit, Job repents in deepest humility. Then, God turns His attention to Job's critics. He states point-blank to Eli, the eldest: *"I am angry with you and your two friends, because you have not spoken the truth about me, as my servant Job has"* (Job 42:7).

When God confronts them, they respond immediately with teachable hearts. God instructs the accusers to bring certain animals to Job which, in turn, become burnt offerings to the Lord. After Job prays for his friends—his former critics—to receive mercy, God promises ...

> **"I will accept his prayer and not deal with you according to your folly."**
> **(Job 42:8)**

In truth, human nature says to react "in kind" to others—insult for insult, blow for blow. However, one of the clearest challenges the Lord gives us is not to react "in kind," but to respond "in the Spirit."

To be Spirit-controlled rather than situation-controlled is not *natural* to human nature. Being Spirit-controlled is *supernatural*, yielding control to the indwelling Holy Spirit, whom you received at salvation. Unmistakably, to return evil for evil is *natural*, but to return good for evil is the *supernatural* response God desires for you to have toward your critics.

Scripture gives a clear directive ...

**"Do not be overcome by evil,
but overcome evil with good."
(Romans 12:21)**

Forgiveness is needed by everyone and is to be extended by everyone, whether requested or not. God commands us to forgive others just as He has forgiven those who are in Christ. However, asking forgiveness of someone and extending forgiveness to someone can be a major stumbling block.

The solution is found in God's Word. He is our masterful Creator, our loving Lord and Savior, our compassionate Ruler and Redeemer. He alone knows our deepest needs, and He alone knows how to meet those needs, including empowering us in the area of forgiveness. His Word to us says ...

**"Bear with each other
and forgive one another
if any of you has a grievance
against someone.
Forgive as the Lord forgave you."
(Colossians 3:13)**

How to Handle "The Hook"

Failing to forgive someone keeps us emotionally "hooked" to that person and reaps negative repercussions in our own lives. Forgiveness involves taking the offender off of our emotional "hook" and putting that person onto God's "hook."

▶ **Make** a list of all the offenses committed against you by your offender.

▶ **Imagine** right now a meat hook around your neck and a burlap bag hanging from the end of the hook resting against your chest.

▶ **Picture** all the pain that is caused by the offenses against you as heavy rocks being dropped into the burlap bag—the greater the pain, the heavier the rocks. So, now you have 100 pounds of rocks—rocks of resentment—hanging from the hook around your neck.

▶ **Ask** yourself, "Do I really want to carry all that pain and resentment the rest of my life? Am I willing to take the pain from the past and release it into the hands of the Lord?"

You can take the one who offended you off of your emotional hook and place your offender onto God's hook. The Lord knows how to deal with your offender in His time and His way. God says ...

"It is mine to avenge; I will repay."
(Deuteronomy 32:35)

PRAYER OF FORGIVENESS

"Lord Jesus, thank You for caring about
how much my heart has been hurt.
You know the pain I have felt
because of (_list every offense_).
Right now I release all that pain
into Your hands.
Thank You, Lord, for dying on the cross for
me and extending Your forgiveness to me.
As an act of my will,
I choose to forgive (_name_).

I take (_name_) off of my emotional hook
and place (_name_) onto your hook.
I refuse all thoughts of revenge.
I trust that in Your time
and in Your way You will
deal with my offender as You see fit.
And Lord, thank You for giving me Your
power to forgive so that I can be set free.
In Your holy name I pray. Amen."

Job's three friends initially come to extend sympathy and comfort, but when they speak, their words are neither sympathetic nor comforting, but confrontational. They violate the first rule of confrontation, which is "confront in private," and Job is offended.

The goal for confrontation is repentance and restoration. Therefore, those who confront inappropriately and those who avoid confrontation altogether do not help the one who needs to change. The detrimental result is that damaging criticism continues and relationships are destroyed.

Jesus stated both the *how* and *why* of confrontation:

"If your brother or sister sins, go and point out their fault, just between the two of you. If they listen to you, you have won them over. But if they will not listen, take one or two others along, so that 'every matter may be established by the testimony of two or three witnesses.'"
(Matthew 18:15–16)

When you must confront ...

▶ **Align** your heart and mind with God's heart.

- Confess any sinful thought, motive, or deed on your part.

- Ask God for discernment and direction as to what, if any, action you are to take.

- Seek God's wisdom through prayer, His Word, and the godly counsel of others.

▶ **Allow** emotions to subside before confronting the problem.

- Realize, reason is not maximized in the heat of the moment.

- Wait until the situation is not contentious before you choose a time to talk.

- Approach the subject calmly and objectively, with a positive, prayerful attitude.

▶ **Acquire** a clear, accurate understanding of the situation before you speak.

- Gather the facts and separate out emotional reactions.

- Listen to objective viewpoints.

- Speak with only those involved.

▶ **Ask** permission before you speak.

- "Could I make a suggestion?"

- "May I make an observation?"

- "I have some thoughts on this situation, if you are interested."

▶ **Assume** responsibility for any wrongful actions on your part.

- "I was wrong to have spoken to you as I did, and I ask your forgiveness."

- "I was wrong to have jumped to a hasty, inaccurate conclusion. I should have gotten all the facts before I formulated any opinion."

- "I was wrong to have taken my anger out on you. Will you please forgive me?"

▶ **Avoid** analyzing another person's feelings or actions.

- Clarify actions: "Tell me, from your perspective, what happened and what you did."

- Identify feelings: "Tell me what you were feeling when (_state what happened_)." "How were you feeling when you . . . ?" "How are you feeling now?"

- Stick to the facts: "I saw you _____." "I understood you to say _____." "If I heard you correctly, you felt _____."

▶ **Apply** the "sandwich approach" in voicing your criticism.

- Give the person the bread of praise: "I appreciate your strong work ethic." "You are a very gifted and competent person." "I recognize that you are a hard worker."

- Add the meat of criticism: "What I need from you right now is for you to speak to me without raising your voice. I feel disrespected and forced into a yelling match in order to resolve our differences."

- Finish with the bread of encouragement: "I am confident you can work with me on this." "I know we can get through this together." "I know you can help me in this way."

▶ **Aim** your criticism at the specific, problematic behavior, not at the person.

- "I appreciate your tremendous efforts, but I am having a problem with the sarcastic comments being made."

- "I enjoy visiting with you, but I need to be able to talk with fewer interruptions so that I can keep my train of thought."

- "I love your sense of humor, but I really don't enjoy off-color jokes and sexual innuendos."

▶ **Abstain** from negative phrases containing "always" or "never."

- Don't say, "You'll *never* change."

- Don't say, "You *always* do this to me."

- Don't say, "You *never* speak to me with respect."

▶ **Address** only one current problematic behavior.

- Don't bring up a list of offenses.

- Don't belabor your point. Simply state it clearly and concisely: "I need you to be truthful with me about (_state the situation_)." "I need you to speak to me in a calm and controlled manner."

- Don't dredge up previously addressed problems.

▶ **Assume** some responsibility for finding a solution to the problem.

- Help formulate a plan for change: "What do you think we need to do?" "How do you think we can resolve this problem together and move on?" "I want to work with you in any way that will be helpful to you."

- Consider the undesirable behavior as the problem, not the person engaging in the behavior. "I'm not looking at this as your problem, but as our problem because it is affecting our relationship. I want us to have the best relationship possible."

- Offer encouragement and emotional support: "What can I do to help?" "What do you need from me?"

▶ **Approach** God together with a united heart.

- Thank God together for His love, grace, and mercy and for the opportunity to honor Him in your relationship.

- Ask God to protect your relationship from petty differences, to guard your communication, and to increase your love for one another.

- Commit to God to be honest, open, and encouraging with one another and to faithfully seek God's wisdom in your decision making.

"Those who trust in themselves are fools, but those who walk in wisdom are kept safe." (Proverbs 28:26)

Job is no insignificant person, as formerly the most renowned man among all the people of the East. But the God of the universe recognizes that his critical spirit needs to be curtailed when it comes to demanding his "day in court."

In reading the book of Job, we can see there is no doubt God delights in what He has created: the earth and its foundation, sea and sky, wind and rain, thunder and lightning, snow and hail, darkness and light, deserts and stars, times and seasons, fish and fowl. His creation now fully put on display before His critical servant Job, God further inquires: *"Who then is able to stand against me? Who has a claim against me that I must pay?"* The obvious answer is—no one! And then God makes a statement that should silence all of His critics, *"Everything under heaven belongs to me"* (Job 41:10–11).

In your own life, think about those who have possessed a critical spirit, whether it's the "tongue-lashing friend" or the "never-satisfied" father or others who wound. They make their "targets" highly vulnerable to others who have a critical spirit.

Therefore, don't let destructive criticism weaken your emotional state. God promises He will bring good from everything—and that includes negative people. For the Christian, one inherent good in any unjust suffering is that it provides the opportunity to emulate Christ's example before the eyes of unbelievers who need to know Him.

> "It is commendable if someone bears up
> under the pain of unjust suffering
> because they are conscious of God. ...
> If you suffer for doing good and you endure
> it, this is commendable before God.
> To this you were called, because Christ
> suffered for you, leaving you an example,
> that you should follow in his steps."
> (1 Peter 2:19–21)

Five Significant Criticizers

#1 CRITICAL PARENTS

QUESTION: "My parents were so critical of me in my childhood that when I became an adult, I withdrew physically and emotionally. I love my parents and have tried reconciliation, but how is this possible when there is no change? Now that I am pregnant, I feel that I must withdraw to protect my child."

ANSWER: You are to be commended for seeking reconciliation even though your parents have not changed. Typically, people do not change unless something motivates them to act differently. Your pregnancy could provide that motivation.

Schedule a time to talk with your parents about the kind of interaction you desire to have with them.

When you are all together ...

▶ **Express** your love and appreciation for them.

▶ **Express** your hurt over their frequent critical words. Give specific examples.

▶ **Express** your strong commitment to create a positive, encouraging environment for your child.

▶ **Express** your decision to spend time with them. Explain your boundary: Either you will leave or they will have to leave if they become negative and critical.

▶ **Express** your resolve to reflect the character and attitude of Christ toward them.

▶ **Express** your desire that they speak lovingly and positively to you and to their grandchild.

Remember, everyone has three God-given inner needs—for love, significance, and security.[9] When we feel like we are lacking in one or more of these areas, we can seek to get these needs met through negative behavior. A critical person is often seeking to meet a deep need for significance. Knowing this, you can seek to encourage and build up your parents in all you say and do.

> **"Let us therefore make every effort
> to do what leads to peace
> and to mutual edification."**
> **(Romans 14:19)**

#2 Critical Spouse

QUESTION: "How can I deal with my critical, perfectionistic spouse? He was raised by a critical mother, and I was raised by a critical father."

ANSWER: Often, a person who is hypercritical has an underlying need to be in control or to feel significant. Your husband may be doing what he knows to do from the modeling he received growing up. Typically, children who grow up with criticism learn to be critical. And children who grow up with encouragement, learn to be encouraging. You cannot expect your husband to copy behavior he has not routinely seen.

▶ **Engage** him in a conversation in which you express your desire for the two of you to break the destructive patterns of interaction you both learned as children.

▶ **Turn** this problem into a project. Both of you must make a commitment to each other and to God to compliment each other about something different each day for the next 12 weeks—writing each compliment down. During these weeks, no words of criticism are to be spoken. Over time, you'll see a positive transformation before your very eyes. And you will both learn to be encouraging and complimentary of one another.

The Bible says ...

"Let us consider how we may spur one another on toward love and good deeds ... "
(Hebrews 10:24)

#3 CRITICAL FRIENDS

QUESTION: "How can I keep from being negatively affected by two verbally abusive people who attack my Christian commitment?"

ANSWER: Realize, you are not the one with a problem. Those being verbally abusive are the ones with the problem.

▶ **Repeat** out loud to yourself three times: "They have a problem. I am not going to let their problem become my problem."

▶ **Rehearse** these two statements every day for two weeks until these truths give you peace and your hurt and anger subside.

▶ **Recognize** their attacks as a reflection of their unmet inner needs.

▶ **Request** that they respect your decision to be a follower of Christ and that they refrain from speaking words of criticism that continue to cause you pain.

▶ **Release** them to God and pray for them to have a life-changing relationship with Him.

▶ **Remember,** Jesus stated that we would be persecuted, but in the midst of persecution, we would be blessed.

"Blessed are you when people hate you, when they exclude you and insult you and reject your name as evil, because of the Son of Man." (Luke 6:22)

#4 CRITICAL MANAGER

QUESTION: "How can I deal with my manager who is excessively critical of me? I feel beat up all the time!"

ANSWER: While we are to honor our authorities and heed their justifiable criticism, we are not called to submit to verbal or emotional abuse. Jesus confronted the religious leaders of His day, but in doing so, He did not have a critical spirit toward them. Prayerfully attempt to draw your supervisor out about your job performance and professional relationship. Humbly ask questions such as ...

▶ Have I offended you in any way?

▶ Is there something I've done that you're displeased with?

▶ In what areas do I need to show improvement?

Your performance review would be an ideal time to raise these questions, but you could also request a private meeting with your manager and say, "I may have a blind spot and don't see what others see. I honestly want to be the very best employee I can be. What could I do to be the greatest asset for our organization? I value your opinion and will work hard to improve." Then listen with an open heart to the answer and bring what you hear before the Lord.

> **"Those who guard their mouths and their tongues keep themselves from calamity."**
> **(Proverbs 21:23)**

#5 CRITICAL CHURCH LEADERS

QUESTION: "Several leaders in my church have judgmental spirits and continually criticize other members. I try to be pleasant and forgiving, but is this the way the leaders in church should act?"

ANSWER: For a spiritual leader to be critical is contrary to Scripture. The Bible says the "shepherds of the flock" are to be humble examples of Christ. Examine yourself and the other people in your church.

Possibly, you are in the wrong church. You could be in a church that is legalistic—one that doesn't allow the grace of God or the love of Christ to flourish. Ask the Lord to lead you in either bringing the matter to a church leader whom you respect or consider finding a new church.

The Bible says ...

**"To the elders among you ...
Be shepherds of God's flock that is under
your care, watching over them—
not because you must,
but because you are willing,
as God wants you to be;
not pursuing dishonest gain,
but eager to serve;
not lording it over those entrusted to you,
but being examples to the flock."
(1 Peter 5:1–3)**

Truth has permeated Job to the core. He is stunned, silenced, and saddened. How impertinent, how insolent, criticizing the Most High God.

To the Almighty, he responds, *"You asked, 'Who is this that obscures my plans without knowledge?' Surely I spoke of things I did not understand, things too wonderful for me to know. ... My ears had heard of you but now my eyes have seen you."* And this revelation prompts an additional admission, *"Therefore I despise myself and repent in dust and ashes"* (Job 42:3, 5–6).

With Job's declaration of repentance, God's heart is moved to befriend and bless. The "greatest man in all the East" becomes even greater, with God bestowing upon him twice as much as he had before—the recipient of double blessing.

God also blesses Job with seven more sons and three daughters—a gift of grace and kindness following the ten who had been previously killed. But it's curious that there isn't a double blessing where Job's children are concerned; there isn't provision for 14 more sons and six more daughters. The subtle message from the Lord: The previous children aren't dead; *they're alive with Him.*

The book of Job teaches much about the dangers of a critical spirit and makes us mindful to pursue having a caring, compassionate spirit.

When critical words come to your mind, you can move in the opposite direction.

Truth That Triumphs over Criticism

The Word of God teaches us that ...

▶ **God provides** mercy, grace, and help in our times of need.

"Let us then approach God's throne of grace with confidence, so that we may receive mercy and find grace to help us in our time of need" (Hebrews 4:16).

▶ **God suffered** for us and bids us to bear the disgrace He bore.

"Jesus also suffered outside the city gate to make the people holy through his own blood. Let us, then, go to him outside the camp, bearing the disgrace he bore" (Hebrews 13:12–13).

▶ **God brought** good from Jesus' bearing the brunt of cynical critics, and He will bring good from unjust criticism aimed at us.

"We know that in all things God works for the good of those who love him, who have been called according to his purpose" (Romans 8:28).

▶ **God secured** our healing from the wounds of criticism by being wounded Himself.

"'He himself bore our sins' in his body on the cross, so that we might die to sins and live for righteousness; 'by his wounds you have been healed'" (1 Peter 2:24).

▶ **Enduring criticism** identifies us with Jesus, who endured criticism for us.

" ... fixing our eyes on Jesus, the pioneer and perfecter of faith. For the joy set before him he endured the cross, scorning its shame, and sat down at the right hand of the throne of God. Consider him who endured such opposition from sinners, so that you will not grow weary and lose heart" (Hebrews 12:2–3).

▶ **Suffering the grief** of unjust criticism proves our faith.

" ... for a little while you may have had to suffer grief in all kinds of trials. These have come so that the proven genuineness of your faith—of greater worth than gold, which perishes even though refined by fire—may result in praise, glory and honor when Jesus Christ is revealed" (1 Peter 1:6–7).

▶ **Finding God's comfort** in the midst of criticism equips us to comfort others.

" ... the Father of compassion and the God of all comfort ... comforts us in all our troubles, so that we can comfort those in any trouble with the comfort we ourselves receive from God. For just as we share abundantly in the sufferings of Christ, so also our comfort abounds through Christ" (2 Corinthians 1:3–5).

▶ **Bearing the pressure** of criticism reveals the life of Christ in us.

"We are hard pressed on every side, but not crushed; perplexed, but not in despair; persecuted, but not abandoned; struck down, but not destroyed. We

*always carry around in our body the death of Jesus,
so that the life of Jesus may also be revealed in our
body"* (2 Corinthians 4:8–10).

▶ **Facing the fiery trial** of criticism perfects
perseverance and leads us to maturity and
completeness of character.

*"Consider it pure joy, my brothers and sisters,
whenever you face trials of many kinds, because
you know that the testing of your faith produces
perseverance. Let perseverance finish its work so
that you may be mature and complete, not lacking
anything"* (James 1:2–4).

Job's Epilogue: The Rest of the Story

Throughout the centuries, Job has been heralded
as a suffering saint. And, indeed, his struggles are
monumental. But so is his reward.

At the conclusion of Job's all-consuming suffering,
along with the critical clamor of his detractors
silenced, the Bible tells us, *"The LORD blessed the
latter part of Job's life more than the former part. ...
After this, Job lived a hundred and forty years; he
saw his children and their children to the fourth
generation. And so Job died, an old man and full
of years"* (Job 42:12, 16–17). Full of fruitful years,
full of tested faith, and full of God's forgiveness.

On this side of eternity, we cannot comprehend
the intricate tapestry God is weaving from the
tormenting threads of criticism that He sovereignly

allows in our lives. However, we can know that, like Job, as we surrender to Him, we will experience the refining of our character and the perfect plan for our lives.

As we learn to tune out all other voices but His, what comfort to find ...

> **"He knows the way that I take;**
> **when he has tested me,**
> **I will come forth as gold."**
> **(Job 23:10)**

To look with a "critical eye" is to pay close attention to detail—and this can be most helpful.

But to look with a "critical spirit" means to microscopically focus on faults—and this is only harmful.

Thus to save us from this sickness, let's see one another as the Lord sees us through the compassionate eyes of Christ.

—June Hunt

SCRIPTURES TO MEMORIZE

Why should I be aware of **the power of the tongue**?

"The tongue has the power of life and death, and those who love it will eat its fruit." (Proverbs 18:21)

Why should we not **pass judgment on someone else**?

"You, therefore, have no excuse, you who pass judgment on someone else, for at whatever point you judge another, you are condemning yourself, because you who pass judgment do the same things." (Romans 2:1)

What is important to know about **building others up**?

"Do not let any unwholesome talk come out of your mouths, but only what is helpful for building others up according to their needs, that it may benefit those who listen." (Ephesians 4:29)

Does God want us to **encourage one another and build each other up**?

"Encourage one another and build each other up." (1 Thessalonians 5:11)

What kind of a person **derides their neighbor**?

"Whoever derides their neighbor has no sense, but the one who has understanding holds their tongue." (Proverbs 11:12)

What enables us to **know how to** appropriately **answer everyone?**

*"Let your conversation be always full of grace, seasoned with salt, so that you may **know how to answer everyone.**"* (Colossians 4:6)

NOTES

1. Timothy Friberg, Barbara Friberg , and Neva F. Miller, *Analytical Lexicon of the Greek New Testament* (Grand Rapids: Baker Books, 2000), #238.

2. *Merriam Webster Online Dictionary*, s.v. "Criticism," http://www.m-w.com.

3. *Merriam Webster Online Dictionary*, s.v. "Care"

4. *The New Shorter Oxford English Dictionary*, vol. 1 ed. Lesley Brown (Oxford: Clarendon Press, 1993), s.v. "Encourage."

5. W. E. Vine, Merrill F. Unger, and William White, *Vine's Complete Expository Dictionary of Biblical Words*, electronic ed. (Nashville: Thomas Nelson, 1996), s.v. "Encourage."

6. Lawrence J. Crabb, Jr., *Understanding People: Deep Longings for Relationship, Ministry Resources Library* (Grand Rapids: Zondervan, 1987), 15–16; Robert S. McGee, *The Search for Significance*, 2nd ed. (Houston, TX: Rapha, 1990), 27–30.

7. Lawrence J. Crabb, Jr. and Dan B. Allender, *Encouragement: The Key to Caring* (Grand Rapids: Zondervan, 1984), 101–21.

8. Crabb, Jr., *Understanding People*, 15–16; McGee, *The Search for Significance*, 27–30.

9. Crabb, Jr., *Understanding People*, 15–16; McGee, *The Search for Significance*, 27–30.

HOPE FOR THE HEART TITLES

www.aspirepress.com